ARCTIC

Explorer

ARCTIC Explorer

The Story of Matthew Henson

Jeri Ferris

Carolrhoda Books, Inc., Minneapolis

For my grandparents
Susan B. and Leon W. Chase

My special thanks to Dr. Joseph Boskin, Boston University, and
Dr. H. Viscount Nelson, Jr., University of California, Los Angeles,
for their generous help and advice.

This edition of this book is available in two bindings:
Library binding by Carolrhoda Books, Inc.
Soft cover by First Avenue Editions
241 First Avenue North
Minneapolis, Minnesota 55401

Library of Congress Cataloging-in-Publication Data

Ferris, Jeri.
    Arctic explorer: the story of Matthew Henson/by Jeri Ferris.
        p. cm.
    Bibliography: p. 76
    Includes index.
    Summary: A biography of the Black explorer who discovered the
North Pole.
    ISBN 0-87614-370-2 (lib. bdg.)
    ISBN 0-87614-507-1 (pbk.)
    1. Henson, Matthew Alexander, 1866-1955—Juvenile literature.
2. Explorers—United States—Biography—Juvenile literature.
3. North Pole—Juvenile literature. | 1. Henson, Matthew Alexander,
1866-1955. 2. Explorers. 3. Afro-Americans—Biography. |
I. Title.
G635.H4F47   1989
919.8'04—dc19
|B|
|92| 88-34449
                                                                 CIP
                                                                  AC

Manufactured in the United States of America

2 3 4 5 6 7 8 9 10 99 98 97 96 95 94 93 92 91 90 89

Contents

Robert Edwin Peary. Peary said he discovered the North Pole on April 6, 1909, but some people believe he never got there at all. The instrument in his right hand is a sextant, which is used in taking solar observations.

Foreword

Did Robert E. Peary and Matthew Henson actually reach the North Pole in April 1909? Ever since 1909 Peary's critics have claimed that he didn't get there at all. The critics say Peary deliberately took an uneducated black man, who wouldn't be able to dispute his observations. They say he didn't let Henson make observations himself, although Henson knew how (Matt wrote, "I can make observations but of course I did not meddle at this time"). They say Peary's own observations were inaccurate. And they say that he returned to the ship far too quickly after Bartlett's last observation to have gone all the way to the Pole and back. The truth may never be known, but *wherever* Peary went, he couldn't have gotten there without Matthew Henson, "the most nearly indispensable man."

At the time of Peary and Henson's explorations of the Arctic, the native people were called "Eskimos" (a Native American word thought to mean "eaters of raw meat") by explorers. However, the native people called themselves "Inuit," which means "the real people," and Inuit is the name preferred today.

Introduction

Matthew Alexander Henson was born in 1866 into a United States of two worlds, a white world and a black world. Matt Henson was black. Robert E. Peary, the man he assisted for 22 years, was white. In the Arctic they ate from the same chunk of frozen walrus; in the United States they did not sit at the same table or even in the same room. In the Arctic they slept in the same igloo; in the United States Henson couldn't enter the same hotel as Peary. In the Arctic they worked side by side, often close to death; in the United States Henson was only Peary's "faithful colored servant." Matt knew this was wrong. His work with Peary, from the equator to the North Pole, proved it.

I
Master of the Sea

Matt stood alone on the docks at Baltimore, looking at the ships that bobbed up and down on the rippling water. He was 14, he was on his own, and he wanted to go to sea. Amid the tangle of spars, he saw a tall three-masted sailing ship with the name *Katie Hines* in gleaming gold letters on its side, bending gracefully in the breeze, pulling gently at its ropes as if anxious to sail away. Matt headed straight for the *Katie Hines,* where he "shipped as a cabin boy on [the] vessel bound for China."

In the morning's first light, Matt stood on deck as the sailors raised and set the sails, one by one. The ropes that held the *Katie Hines* fast to the dock were pulled on board and carefully coiled up, each in its own place. Slowly at first, the sails caught the wind and billowed out, and the *Katie Hines* set off for China.

Matt easily learned his job as cabin boy (keep Captain Childs's room in order, serve his meals, wash the dishes, help the cook), and he started on other skills. He learned how to build sea chests and sleeping bunks from the ship's carpenter. He learned how to repair engines and rudders and winches from the ship's mechanic. He learned basic navigation from Captain Childs. In his five years on the *Katie Hines,* Matt became an "able-bodied seaman." He sailed from China to Japan to the Philippines; across the Atlantic to France, Africa, and southern Russia; and through the Arctic to Murmansk.

In short, Matt Henson became a master of the sea.

And he mastered more than the sea. Captain Childs had books on geography, history, mathematics, and literature—especially Dickens and Shakespeare. Matt had gone to school in Washington, D.C., but only through the sixth grade, and this wasn't enough for him. So he studied in the captain's library, with Captain Childs as his teacher. The captain taught Matt about people and places and dates, he taught Matt to respect himself and others, and he taught him to be a man who proved his worth by his work.

Then Captain Childs died and was buried at sea. When the *Katie Hines* returned to Baltimore, Matt resigned. He was 19 and on his own again.

Matt tried to find work that would use his expert skills, but he soon learned that it wasn't his skills that mattered, it was his color. He was the wrong color. So he drifted, off course like a rudderless ship, from town to town, job to job. He was a stevedore, a valet, a messenger boy, a night watchman. Finally he returned to Washington, where he found a job as a stock clerk at the clothing and hat store of B. H. Steinmetz and Sons.

, At about that time Lieutenant Robert E. Peary, who was exactly 10 years older than Matt Henson, was looking for a hat. Peary had set his goal in life—"I shall not be satisfied that I have done my best," he wrote his mother, "until my name is known from one end of the earth to the other." He planned to start making his name known by leading the first expedition across Greenland, a huge piece of unexplored and mostly ice-covered land just below the North Pole. He would cross the narrow southern end. This was the shortest way across, but it was still forbiddingly dangerous. And Peary had a dream, as well. He said that the discoverer of the North Pole would be as famous as Christopher Columbus. He, Peary, might someday become that discoverer.

But that was not why he needed a hat. Instead of going north, he was going south to Nicaragua. Peary was an engineer in the United States Navy, and his job was to find the best place to dig a canal across Nicaragua to connect the Atlantic and Pacific oceans. Nicaragua is in the tropics, so Peary needed a tropical helmet. He went into B. H. Steinmetz for his hat.

Matt Henson and Robert Peary looked at each other across the counter. Matt saw a tall, lean red-haired man with sharp blue-gray eyes. Under Peary's long,

Henson and Peary in Nicaragua in 1888. As it turned out, the canal was not built in Nicaragua but in Panama. The Panama Canal was completed in 1914.

straight nose, a shaggy mustache swept out to drooping ends. Peary saw a determined young black man with a calm, steady gaze, and he knew that he had found a helper as well as a hat.

In November 1887 Matt, as Peary's body servant, sailed with 45 engineers and 100 black Jamaican laborers to Nicaragua. They set to work the day they arrived. The engineers surveyed, the laborers chopped down trees, and Matt kept the jungle camp in order.

Seven months later, in summer 1888, the survey was done. Peary had watched Matt's work, and as they sailed back to New York, he told Matt about his goal to lead the first expedition to cross Greenland's ice cap. He asked if Matt would go with him, as his servant and helper. Matt quickly agreed because, he said, "I recognized in [Peary] the qualities that made me willing to engage myself in his service." ⌐

Matt returned to work at Steinmetz's store in Washington while Peary set out to raise money for the expedition to Greenland. In September 1889 Peary was still trying to raise money when an article about Greenland appeared in the paper. Another man, Fridtjof Nansen of Norway, had just crossed the ice cap. Matt's hopes fell. No one would put up money for the second expedition to cross Greenland.

Then in January 1891 Matt received a letter from Peary. He told Matt he had a new plan for Greenland, a better plan, and there was a job for Matt at the League Island Navy Yard in Philadelphia, where Peary was working.

When Matt arrived, Peary explained his plan. True, Nansen had crossed the narrow southern end of Greenland, but the wide northern end was still unexplored. Now Peary intended to be the first to go there. In fact, he had a much grander plan than that. Northern Greenland might actually go all the way to the North Pole, and now, just as he had dreamed, Peary planned to be the first one *there* too.

Peary had enough money to hire a ship and equipment for the North Greenland Expedition. Unfortunately, said Peary, there was no money to pay Matt. Would he go anyway?

Matt did not hesitate. He told Peary he'd be proud to help him on this expedition, with or without pay.

II
The First North Greenland Expedition

"It was in June, 1891," Matt Henson wrote, "that I started on my first trip to the Arctic regions, as a member of what was known as the 'North Greenland Expedition.'"

America's newspapers predicted disaster. A small group of inexperienced men trying to survive in a frozen place that had killed better men than they? Impossible. Then reporters learned that a woman was going too—the new Mrs. Peary. "Now we know he's crazy!" said one newspaper about Peary.

Josephine Peary listed the expedition members in her diary: "Dr. Cook, Mr. Gibson, Mr. Astrup, Mr. Verhoeff, and Mr. Peary's faithful colored attendant in his surveying labors in Nicaragua, Matt Henson." The ship, *Kite,* was so small that the people and supplies barely fit. They were going to be gone for a year and a half, so they needed a lot of supplies.

Members of the 1891-1892 North Greenland Expedition (left to right): Cook, Henson, Astrup, Verhoeff, and Gibson. Josephine and Robert Peary are standing in back. John Verhoeff fell into a crevasse in Greenland in the spring of 1892 while exploring and was never seen again.

There were crates of food (enough for two and a half years, just to be safe) and cans of pemmican, the beef-fat-raisin mixture that the men and dogs would eat while crossing the ice cap. There were skis and snowshoes, guns and ammunition, sledges, woolen clothing, a stove, pots and pans, and camera equipment. And after the last one hundred tons of coal was piled on deck, Matt could hardly find a place to set down his hammer and nails while he put together the wood frame for their base camp house.

The *Kite* plunged on through the Atlantic, rolling

and pitching and sending all the passengers except Henson and Peary to bed seasick. On June 21 Matt saw Greenland for the first time. Its steep, wild cliffs rose straight up from the icy water. As the *Kite* steamed north through Baffin Bay, Matt saw hundreds of icebergs—gleaming blue and white chunks of ice— from the size of small sailboats to that of enormous floating mountains. In the valleys of Greenland, Matt saw glaciers that looked like thick flowing cream, frozen into white walls. And on the very top of Greenland lay the five hundred thousand square miles of silent ice cap. Matt couldn't see it yet, but he knew it was there, waiting.

The *Kite* pushed farther north into heavy ice, which floated on the water like a field of white. There were splits and cracks in the ice, and through these cracks (called leads) the *Kite* forced its way. Sometimes there were no leads at all, and the captain would shout for more steam power. The *Kite* would dash forward and smash against the ice. Sometimes the ice would break, and the ship could continue. Sometimes it would not, and the ship would have to back up and try another way.

When the *Kite* was as far north as it could go, it dropped anchor in McCormick Bay, Greenland, and the crew unloaded the supplies. At the end of July, the *Kite* sailed for home, leaving Matthew Henson, the Pearys, and the other four men to survive the arctic winter. (A ship could only get through the ice in the summer, and the long, dangerous trip over the ice cap could only be started in the spring with the return of 24-hour sunlight. So the men had to wait in the Arctic through the dark winter months.) Matt immediately began putting up their sturdy house, to make sure they would survive.

August 8 was Matt's 25th birthday. For the first time in his life, he had a birthday celebration. Mrs. Peary fixed mock turtle soup, stew of little auk (a bird the size of a robin) with green peas, eider duck, baked beans, corn, tomatoes, and apricot pie. Matt remembered the delight of that dinner long after the tin plates were put away. Seventeen years later he said of that day, "To have a party given in my honor touched me deeply."

While Matt finished the small wooden house, the other men went to find Eskimos to join their group. (The men would have to use sign language because none of them spoke Eskimo.) Peary needed Eskimo men to help hunt polar bears and seals and walruses and reindeer and caribou and foxes for furs and meat. He needed Eskimo women to chew the furs and sew them into pants and coats. The thickest wool coat from home would be useless in the Arctic; they had to have clothing made of the same fur that kept the arctic animals warm. In exchange for their work, Peary would give the Eskimos pots and pans, needles, tools, and other useful items.

On August 18 the men returned, and with them were four Eskimos: Ikwa, his wife, and their two children. The Eskimos walked slowly up to Matt and the Pearys. Then Ikwa stepped closer to Matt and looked at him carefully. His brown face lit up with excitement as he spoke rapidly to Matt in Eskimo. Matt shook his head and tried to explain that he didn't understand, but Ikwa kept talking. Finally Ikwa took Matt's arm, pointed at the black man's skin, and said, "Inuit, Inuit!" Then Matt understood. "Inuit" must be what the Eskimos called themselves. Ikwa thought Matt was another Eskimo because he had brown skin, just as the Eskimos did. Matt looked down at the short fur-covered man, who smelled like seals and whale blubber. He looked into Ikwa's shining black eyes and smiled. From that moment on, the Eskimos called Matt "Miy Paluk," which meant "dear little Matthew," and they loved him as a brother.

In September Matt, Ikwa, Dr. Cook, and the Pearys took the whale boat and went to find more Eskimos. They didn't find a single Eskimo, but they did find some unfriendly walruses.

It began when the boat got mixed up with some walruses (250 walruses, Mrs. Peary said) that were peacefully fishing for clams. One after another the startled walruses poked their heads out of the water, spitting out clam shells and flashing their white tusks. Then an angry bull walrus roared, "Ook, ook, ook!" and headed straight for the boat. The water foamed and boiled as the rest of the herd charged right behind him, speeding along like torpedoes, all roaring their battle cry and tossing their enormous gray wrinkled heads. Matt and the others knew that just one tusk through the bottom of the boat would be the end of them. Ikwa shouted and pounded on the boat to frighten the walruses away, but the walruses weren't frightened. In fact, they were so angry that they tossed the boat up and down furiously. Bracing their feet, Matt and the others fired their guns while Mrs. Peary sat in the bottom of the boat and reloaded the guns as fast as she could. At last the walruses gave up. They dove to the bottom and disappeared, leaving a shaky group of explorers in a still-rocking boat.

By the end of September, the dull red sun dipped lower each day and finally did not appear at all over the southern horizon. Every day was like a glorious sunset, with a golden, crimson glow on the mountain peaks. Then there was no sunset anymore, just one long night.

By the time the sun was gone, not to return until February, several Eskimo families were living at the camp in stone igloos (snow igloos were only used when the Eskimos traveled, following the animals whose meat and skins they needed).

That winter the men hunted by the full moon—by moonlight so bright that the blue-white ice sparkled. Peary planned for the spring trek. Astrup taught the men to ski. Gibson studied bird and animal life. Verhoeff studied rocks. Dr. Cook *wanted* to study the Eskimos by taking their pictures and measuring their bodies, but the Eskimos refused to let him near them. Finally Matt realized that they were afraid Dr. Cook would go home and make new people from the

Matt and an Eskimo friend return from a hunting expedition. The Eskimos could not pronounce the word "Matt," so they called Henson "Miy."

Eskimo pattern. So Matt got Ikwa to understand, and Dr. Cook got his pictures.

Meanwhile Matt studied with his Eskimo teachers. They taught him easy things, such as never to stand with his feet apart or his elbows sticking out, as this let the cold air close to his body. They taught him hard things, such as how to speak Eskimo. Matt learned, for example, that there is no Eskimo word for "hole." Instead there is a different word for "hole in igloo" or "hole in bear skin" or anything that has a hole.

Matt learned why the Eskimos smelled like walruses and seals and blubber—they *ate* walruses and seals and blubber. They also ate reindeer and polar bears and little auks. They ate the meat while it was still warm and raw and bloody; they ate it when it was frozen solid, by chopping off bite-size chunks; and sometimes they boiled it. They never ate carrots or beans or potatoes or apples or chocolate. In the Arctic the only food came from the bodies of the animals that lived there.

Matt learned how the Eskimos made the skin of a polar bear into clothing. Once the Eskimo man had killed the bear and removed its skin and scraped it as clean as he could, it was up to the Eskimo woman to finish. She had to chew the skin until all the fat was gone and it was completely soft. All day long the woman would fold the skin (with the fur folded inside), chew back and forth along the fold, make a new fold, and continue. It took two days to chew one skin. Then the woman would rest her jaws for one day before beginning on another skin. After the skin had dried, she would cut it up and sew it into a coat or pants. Her needle was made of bone, her thread was made from animal sinew, and her stitches had to be very, very tiny so not a whisper of wind could get through.

For Matt's winter outfit the women made stockings of arctic hare fur, tall boots of sealskin, polar bear fur pants, a shirt made of 150 auk skins (with the feathers next to Matt's skin), a reindeer fur jacket, and a white fox fur hood that went around his face. His mittens were made of bearskin with the fur inside.

An Eskimo woman makes clothing out of an animal skin. Old Eskimo women had very short, flat teeth from chewing skins to soften them.

But the piercing, freezing cold, colder than the inside of a freezer, took Matt's breath away, and the howling arctic wind drove needles of snow and ice into his face. Even his new sealskin boots felt terrible, until he learned to stand still after he put them on in the morning. Then they would freeze instantly to the shape of his feet and wouldn't hurt as much.

Once Matt had his fur clothes, cold or not, he was ready to learn how to drive a sledge pulled by the 80- to 120-pound Eskimo dogs. But first, if a dog got loose, Matt had to catch him. He would drop a piece of frozen meat on the snow and dive on top of the dog as the animal snatched the meat. Then he would "grab the nearest thing grabbable—ear, leg, or bunch of hair," slip the harness over the dog's head, push his front legs through, and tie him to a rock. Finally, Matt said, he would lick his dog bites.

When the dogs were in their traces, they spread out like a fan in front of the sledge. The king dog, who was the strongest and fiercest, led the way in the center. Matt had watched the Eskimos drive the dogs and knew that they didn't use the 30-foot sealskin whip *on* the dogs but *over* the dogs. The trick was to make the whip curl out and crack like a gunshot right over the ear of the dog who needed it. Matt stepped up behind the sledge, shouted, "Huk, huk!" and tried to crack the whip. The dogs sat down. Matt tried again and again and again. After many tries and lots of help from his Eskimo teachers, Matt learned how to snap the whip over the dogs' ears and make them start off at a trot. Then he had to learn how to turn them (they didn't have reins, as horses do), how to make them stop, and how to make them jump over open water with the sledge flying behind.

There were five Eskimo families at the camp, each family with its own stone igloo. At first it was hard for Matt to go inside the igloos because of their peculiar smell (Eskimos did not take baths, and Matt said that an Eskimo mother cleans her baby just as a mother cat cleans her kittens), but he didn't want to be rude, so he got used to it. Opposite the entrance hole was the bed platform, built of stone and covered with furs. At the end of the bed platform was a small stone lamp, filled with whale blubber for fuel, with moss for the wick. This little lamp was the light and heat and cook stove for the igloo. The Eskimo woman melted snow in a small pan over the lamp and used the water for cooking meat and for drinking. (Eskimos did not build fires for heating or cooking.)

Matt learned how to build a snow igloo when he hunted with the Eskimos, far from the camp. Two Eskimos could cut 50 to 60 snow blocks (each block 6-by-18-by-24-inches) with their long snow knives and build a whole igloo in just one hour. One man would stand in the center and place the blocks in an 8-foot circle around himself. He would add more blocks, spiraling round and round, with the blocks closing in on the center as they rose higher, until the top snow blocks fit perfectly against each other and the roof was complete. Then they would carry in the furs and cooking lamp, and it was home. A chunk of frozen meat, perhaps part of a walrus, might be in the middle of the igloo, handy for snacks and also a good footstool. Snow igloos even had shelves. The Eskimos would stick their snowshoes into the wall and lay mittens on the snowshoe shelf to dry.

The dogs, who had thick silver gray or white hair with a layer of short fine fur underneath to keep them warm, lived outdoors in the snow. They would curl into balls, cover their noses with their tails, and sleep, warm as muffins (usually), even if it was −50°F.

Above, dogs in their traces fan out in front of a sledge. If they are starving, the dogs will eat their traces, which are made of sealskin. Below, dogs curl up outside Peary's igloo.

During the full moons Matt and the Eskimos hunted reindeer and arctic hares. The large pure white hares themselves could not be seen against the white snow, only their black shadows. They were like an army of frozen or leaping ghosts. And in the deep blackness of the arctic night, Matt saw hundreds of shooting stars, so thick and close they seemed to burst like rockets. While he watched the stars, the Eskimos explained that what Matt called the Big Dipper was really seven reindeer eating grass, and the constellation he called the Pleiades was really a team of dogs chasing a polar bear.

The Eskimos had no tables or chairs, no books or paper or writing, no money or bills to pay, no king or chief, no doctors or dentists, no schools or churches, no laws, and no wars. They needed shelter from the cold, strong dogs to pull their sledges, and animals they could hunt for furs and meat. Several families usually lived close together to help each other. If one man killed a walrus, he would share it with everyone. Perhaps in a few days another man would kill a bear or a reindeer; then that man would share it too.

Meanwhile in the wooden house, there was more to eat than raw meat, and there was a new cook. Mrs. Peary wrote in her diary for November 17, 1891, "Matt got supper tonight, and will from now until May 1 prepare all the meals under my supervision." For Christmas, at least, he didn't do all the cooking. Mrs. Peary prepared arctic hare pie with green peas, reindeer with cranberry sauce, corn and tomatoes, plum pudding, and apricot pie. Then, wrote Mrs. Peary, "Matt cleared everything away."

In February the sun returned. For days and days before it actually appeared, the sky was a magnificent dawn of pink, blue, crimson, and deep yellow, with rosy clouds. Then the sun appeared in the south at noon, but just for a moment the first day. Each day it rose a little higher. The crystal clear water in the bay was deep blue, and the air was thick with the sound of wings and songs as thousands of birds swooped and swarmed over the water and up the cliffs.

But Greenland's ice cap, which Matt intended to cross, was a frozen, lifeless desert of snow and howling wind and glaciers and deep crevasses. Even though Matt always covered the inside of his boots with soft dried moss for insulation, his heel froze when he helped haul boxes of pemmican and biscuits up to the ice cap in the beginning of May. (Freezing is very serious. The blood stops moving in the frozen part, and the skin and muscle can soon die.) Matt, who was the best at driving the dogs and at speaking the Eskimo language, had planned to be one of the first men to cross the ice cap, but Peary sent him back to the base camp. There were three reasons: one was the frozen heel; another was that someone had to protect Mrs. Peary at the camp; and the third was that Peary believed an explorer should have a college education in order to know what to do in an emergency.

During the short summer, while the others were gone, Matt went hunting so everyone would have plenty of fresh meat; he learned more of the Eskimo language; his foot healed; and he protected Mrs. Peary from danger.

In the end only Peary and Astrup actually crossed the ice cap. All the others turned back. The Eskimos, who feared Kokoyah, the evil spirit of the ice cap, refused to go at all. Peary did discover a large bay at the northeast corner of Greenland, which he named Independence Bay, but he did not find out if there was a way to get to the North Pole by land. He would have to try again. He asked Matt to come along again too.

On September 24, 1892, the first North Greenland Expedition returned to New York to the hurrahs and welcomes of excited Americans. Peary was famous. Matt was hardly noticed. But Peary knew how important Matt was. He wrote, "Henson, my faithful colored boy, a hard worker and apt at anything, . . . showed himself . . . the equal of others in the party."

Peary received many congratulations for his crossing of northern Greenland, including one from Norway's Nansen, who had crossed Greenland first. Then Peary learned, to his dismay, that *Nansen* wanted to be first to discover the North Pole. Peary needed to raise money quickly for his next trip.

In January 1893 Matt Henson and Peary and six Eskimo dogs set out on a three-month speaking tour. An Eskimo tent and furs were spread out on the stage while Peary described Eskimo and arctic life. Then the audience heard "Huk, huk!" and out raced the dogs with Matt in his furs behind the sledge, cracking his whip. The dogs knew how long the program should last, and if Peary talked too long, they would begin to howl. This ended the program. Lots of people wanted to see Henson and hear Peary, and by March there was enough money for the next expedition to Greenland.

III
Kokoyah:
The Spirit
of the Ice Cap

For his second try Peary hired the ship the *Falcon* and took a larger group of men — 12 in all, counting Peary. Except for Henson and Astrup, they were all new men. Then there were Mrs. Peary, who was expecting a baby in September, and a nurse. There were also two St. Bernard dogs, eight burros, and many crates of homing pigeons. (The burros and pigeons didn't last long. Matt said the "burros from Colorado . . . did not make good, making better dog-food instead." The unfortunate homing pigeons didn't make good either. They got lost or froze to death or vanished in one snap of a dog's teeth.) The *Falcon* sailed from Philadelphia on June 26, 1893. Nansen sailed from Norway on the very same day.

Before the darkness of the arctic winter closed in, Matt and the others tried to put supply caches of food out on the ice cap. But blinding ice storms froze their fingers and wrenched away their sledges. Matt shook with fear and cold and helplessness as the howling wind hurled boxes and huge stone boulders over the cliffs. "I have been there," Matt said about those storms, "and believe me, I have been afraid." The Eskimos said the storms were Kokoyah's work.

Matt expected to be included in the 1894 spring trek across the ice cap. With his skills, he knew he would be a valuable member of the expedition. But he was not included. Peary still believed that the best explorer was the college-educated explorer.

On March 6 Peary and his men left; on April 20 they returned. They had gone only 128 miles, and half the dogs had either gone mad or frozen to death in the ice storms. The expedition had failed, but they had left a huge cache of supplies 128 miles out on the ice cap for the next try.

While Peary and the others recovered, Matt was given a little orphaned Eskimo boy to care for. Eskimo children were greatly loved and there weren't many of them, so this was a great honor for Matt. He brought Kudlooktoo into the house, burned his dirty fur clothes, cut his hair, gave him the first bath of his life, and "made him a presentable Young American."

Matt knew the men blamed Peary for the failure of the expedition, and although the *Falcon* was not due back for another year, Peary was afraid it would come early. Then the news of his failure would be carried back to the States, and all of his men would probably return as well. He would be finished as an explorer.

Matt in his furs, holding a baby musk ox

So Peary came up with another plan. There were rumored to be three "iron mountains" somewhere not too far from the camp. Peary found the iron mountains, actually three huge meteorites, and he marked them with a *P.* Later he would dig them up and take them to the United States.

On July 31, 1894, as Peary had feared, the *Falcon* returned one year early. And, as he had feared, every single man on the expedition rushed to get on the ship and go home—every man, that is, except Matt Henson and Hugh Lee. Peary was determined to cross to the northeast corner of Greenland and go to the North Pole from there, and Matt Henson was determined to go with him. Lee decided to go along too. Peary wrote in his diary, "Lee and Henson alone possessed the grit and loyalty to remain." The *Falcon* sailed on August 26 with Peary's unhappy men, Mrs. Peary and the baby, and the news that Peary had found the iron mountains.

Matt found his third arctic winter filled with "gorgeous bleakness, beautiful blackness." Moonlight made a fairyland of the dark valleys, glistening snow, and deep, deep silence. In the spring, as the sun returned, the air became a pearly mist, with huge billowy clouds of pink and purple and gold filling the sky.

On April 1, 1895, Henson, Peary, and Lee left their camp with 3 Eskimos, 6 sledges loaded with walrus meat, and 60 dogs. They planned to find the pemmican Peary had left on the ice cap the year before, cross the ice cap, and go all the way to the North Pole.

The weather was clear and warm, only −14°F, and the silent, frozen ice field was blindingly white in the sun, as if sprinkled with diamond dust. When they got to the spot where the supplies had been left, they searched and dug, but they found nothing. Peary wrote, "All my essential supplies were . . . forever buried in the . . . 'Great Ice.'"

Now they had to decide whether to turn back or take a chance with death and go on over the ice cap with just frozen walrus to eat. (Pemmican had the sugar and fat needed for energy and was not too heavy to carry. Walrus meat didn't provide much energy and weighed four times more.) There would be no living thing on the ice cap except for the men and their dogs. If there were no musk oxen or reindeer to hunt on the other side of the ice cap, or if their food ran out before they got there, then they would die. Matt Henson and Hugh Lee were both willing to take the chance, but the Eskimos turned back.

Henson, Peary, and Lee had gone only 15 miles when Lee got sick. Henson and Peary stopped and put up the tent (there wasn't enough snow on the ice cap to build an igloo), and Lee crawled inside. That left two men to feed the half-wild dogs, and "to keep a pack of 40 ravenous Eskimo dogs in order during feeding time," Peary wrote, "is something beyond the power of two men." They managed to get the dogs tied to stakes pounded in the ice, and Peary walked around with his whip trying to keep them in order while Matt chopped up the frozen walrus meat. But

Matt repairs a sledge on the Greenland ice cap in 1895.

the dogs pulled their stakes loose and attacked the walrus meat and Henson and Peary too. The men leaped out of the pack of fighting, snarling dogs before their boots could be eaten.

Two days later there was a terrible storm. The men huddled together in the tent, with the wind flattening the tent walls right on top of them. When the storm had passed, they started off again. No matter how hungry the men were, it was hard to bite off the frozen raw meat, and when they tried to chew the meat, it cut the insides of their mouths. If they tried to soften it in warm tea, the very sight of the slippery raw chunks made them sick. Each day they went slower as they got weaker and weaker.

By the end of April there wasn't much walrus meat left, so the men had to kill the weakest dogs and feed them to the dogs who could still pull. By early May there were only 17 dogs left. A few days later there were only 11. And then they were at the edge of the ice cap. They slid and scrambled down the cliffs to the valley, where they found musk oxen tracks. Lee, who was too weak to go on, stayed behind with the starving dogs.

Henson and Peary took their rifles and followed the oxen tracks. They found 22 musk oxen, peacefully eating dried moss and grass. Silently the two men crept toward the animals until they were close enough to shoot, and before the herd fled, several oxen lay dead. With his last bullet Matt killed an ox that was charging straight for Peary. The ox fell only 12 feet from Peary.

Matt hurried back for Lee and the dogs, singing all the way. Lee wrote in his diary for May 18, "This is the fourth day that Lt. Peary and Matt have been away. . . ." On May 19 he wrote, "Last night, a little before midnight, I heard Matt's voice singing . . . the sweetest song I ever heard."

They skinned the oxen and cut out warm, bloody chunks of meat, eating it as they worked, throwing huge pieces to the dogs. Peary was right, Matt thought, when he said an explorer needed a good heart, a strong stomach, and an optimistic nature.

The men continued walking northeast until they stood at the edge of sheer cliffs looking out over

Independence Bay, four thousand feet below, and across to mountains stretching north. Peary had planned to climb down the cliffs, cross the bay, and find out if the mountains were on islands that led to the North Pole. But no matter where they looked, there was no way down those cliffs—no way to get to the Pole. Even if they had found a way down, it would not have been possible to go on with their one tattered sledge and nine exhausted dogs. Now it might not be possible to return either.

They started back on June 1, carrying as much fresh meat as their sledge would hold. It wasn't enough. By the time they were halfway across the ice cap, only four dogs were left. But somehow the men survived, and they arrived at the base camp on June 25 with one dog left. Matthew Henson was not only the first black person to cross Greenland but one of the few people who had ever crossed it.

Years later Matt wrote that of all his memories, "the recollections of the long race with death across the 450 miles of the ice-cap of North Greenland in 1895, with Commander Peary and Hugh Lee, are still the most vivid."

Henson, Peary, and Lee slept and ate through the whole month of July, fed by the Eskimos on fresh meat and bowls and bowls of seals' blood. Actually, only Matt was brave enough to drink the thick, warm, dark red blood; Peary and Lee couldn't do it. The seals' blood worked, and on July 15 Matt felt so good he baked a cake for Peary and Lee.

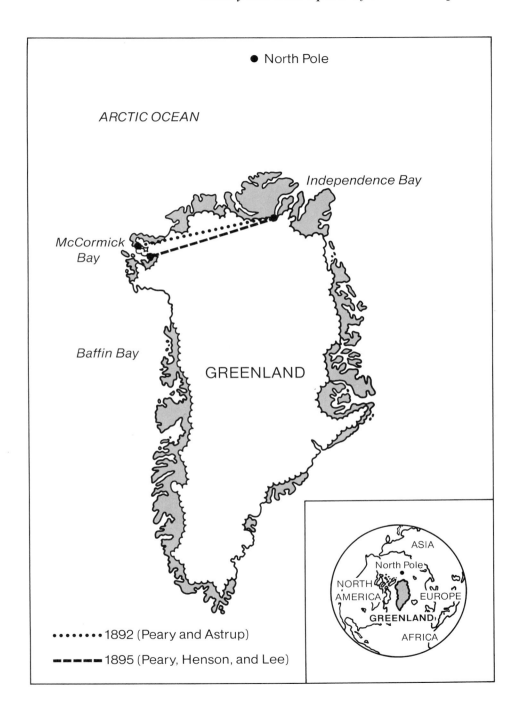

On August 3, 1895, the ship *Kite* arrived to take them home. Peary had to have something to show for his two years in Greenland, so he got two of the meteorites on board the small wooden ship. Meanwhile Matt was busy with several dead walruses. He carefully skinned them and prepared the hides for display at the American Museum of Natural History in New York.

When the *Kite* docked in New York, the curator of the museum was so impressed with the preparation of the walrus skins that he offered Matt a job. Matt accepted, and for the next two years he worked on exhibits of arctic life. He took time off during the summers of 1896 and 1897 to go with Peary to the Arctic to bring back the largest meteorite, finally succeeding in 1897.

In 1896 news came that Nansen had gotten to within 225 miles of the North Pole, the closest anyone had ever been, before giving up. Nansen intended to try again, and now a *third* man, Otto Sverdrup of Norway, was headed for the North Pole. Meanwhile Peary had another plan. Since there was no land route to the North Pole, he would walk to the Pole over the frozen Arctic Ocean (that is, he thought he would). He planned to stay in the Arctic for four years if necessary, until he got to the Pole. He asked Matt to come along as his assistant.

Matt had a difficult decision to make. He had a well-respected job at the museum, a job that used his intelligence and skills, and he had some fine friends.

But Matt also wanted to bring honor to his people. He knew that Peary was determined to discover the North Pole, and he believed that by assisting Peary in this discovery, he would bring great honor and pride to all black Americans. So Matt decided to return to the Arctic with Peary and persevere until the Pole was won.

This time Peary chose only one other man, a doctor, to go with them. (Dr. Dedrick and Peary did not get along, and Dedrick did not stay the entire four years.) Peary knew now that he had been wrong to believe only a college-educated person could think well enough to survive in the Arctic. Matt Henson had proven to be better than any of the others.

IV
Tornasuk: The Spirit of the Frozen Sea

On July 4, 1898, the ship *Windward* left New York. A few weeks later it was trapped in heavy ice, still 300 miles south of the Arctic Ocean and 700 miles from the North Pole. They unloaded their supplies on Ellesmere Island, but they were much too far south.

That winter Peary decided to move 250 miles north on the island to Fort Conger, an old abandoned camp. He was afraid to wait until the sun returned because Sverdrup might have the same idea. They would have to go now and claim the camp at Fort Conger — whatever the cost.

So, following the coastline, lifting and pushing their sledges over smashed ice blocks day after day in total darkness, in terrible cold, Henson and Peary and the Eskimos arrived at Fort Conger in January 1899. Sverdrup was not there.

Explorers of the Arctic face more obstacles than just cold and darkness. Above, expedition members lift and push their sledges over ice blocks. Below, an ice floe is being used as a ferry across a narrow lead.

But when Peary pulled off his boots, his feet were as white as marble statues and just as lifeless. Matt quickly placed Peary's frozen feet on his own warm bare stomach and rubbed them to try to bring the blood circulation back. After an hour Peary's feet looked better, except for his toes, which were turning black. Then a fierce storm swept over the cabin, trapping the men. Matt kept the fire going and fed and cared for Peary. Finally, on February 18 when the storms stopped, he placed Peary gently on a sledge, wrapped furs around him, and set off for the ship. There, all of Peary's toes except the two little ones were amputated.

That spring Peary practiced walking on ice and snow with no toes. (He walked with a slide, Matt said.) They would not be able to get to the North Pole in 1899, but there were three years left.

In April 1900 Henson and Peary crossed from Ellesmere Island to Greenland, looking for a jumping-off point toward the Pole. The Eskimos were terrified at being so close to the great ocean, whose devil, Tornasuk, they believed was even more cruel than Kokoyah of the ice cap. And when they heard the groaning of the ice as the ocean moved under it, they were sure of it. Peary found he could not get to the North Pole from Greenland. Now there were two years left.

In the spring of 1901, Henson and Peary went straight north on Ellesmere Island to Cape Hecla, on the north coast. But that year the sea ice was pushed and piled into mountains that could not be climbed over or cut through. They could not get to the North Pole in 1901. Now there was one year left.

On April 6, 1902, with four Eskimos, Henson and Peary left the land at Cape Hecla and stepped onto the frozen Arctic Ocean. Matt quickly saw why the Eskimos so feared the great devil of the frozen sea. As terrible as it had been to cross the Greenland ice cap, at least that had been solid land. Now they were on a movable ice cap, one that cracked open right under their feet—an ice cap that turned into ice floes that floated loose, swirling in icy black water. The ice was like a living thing, lifting and sinking under their feet, thundering like an angry walrus, roaring like a mad polar bear, groaning like a dying whale. And as it moved, the ice folded and crumbled, lifting into enormous mountains of ice blocks, like houses piled on top of one another.

They often came to leads, the rivers of open water where the ice had split apart. Then they would have to wait until the ice jammed together again and dash across it before it opened; or find an ice floe large enough to hold the sledge and the dogs and use it as a ferry from one side to the other; or wait until new ice formed over the water and pray it would hold their weight. If the lead was narrow enough, they could unharness the dogs and use the sledge as a bridge.

Matt led the way, searching for places to cross the leads and the mountains of ice blocks. They struggled north for two weeks. Then on April 21 they came to a lead more than a mile wide. They could not cross it, and they didn't have enough food to wait for the ice to close. Henson and Peary had reached 84°16′ north latitude, an American record for "farthest north," but it was not the Pole (the North Pole is at 90° north latitude). They were only 343 miles from the North Pole, but they had to turn back again. That night Peary wrote in his diary, "I cannot accomplish the impossible."

On August 5, 1902, the *Windward* returned for them, and Henson and Peary returned to the United States. Henson was now 36 and Peary was 46. They had worked together for 15 years. "[We] had every experience, except death," Matt wrote, "and more than once we looked death squarely in the face."

Even though Peary had failed to reach the Pole, he was praised by President Theodore Roosevelt and honored with gold medals for setting the American record for farthest north (the Norwegian explorer Nansen had been farther). Peary began work on yet another expedition, this time planning to use a ship strong enough to cut its way through the ice all the way to the Arctic Ocean. He worked on his new plan until 1905.

Meanwhile Matt had to find another job. He decided to see the United States by train and was hired as a porter on the Pennsylvania Railroad. Before he left New York, the black community of Harlem gave a party for him. At the party Matt met a bright young woman named Lucy Ross. Matt and Lucy took long walks and had long talks every time Matt returned to New York. Before long Matt decided that at last he had found the woman he wanted to marry. But first he had one more trip to make.

On July 16, 1905, Henson and Peary sailed north again, this time on a brand-new ship, the *Roosevelt,* built specially for smashing through the arctic ice. It was a small ship—only 35½ feet wide, the width of a classroom, and 184 feet long, the width of a football field. It had a tremendously strong frame of oak and steel and enough engine and sail power for three ships. It had a sharp bow (front) to cut through the ice and an egg-shaped bottom so the ship would pop up out of the ice when squeezed, instead of being crushed. On board were three other assistants: Bob Bartlett, who was also captain of the *Roosevelt;* Ross Marvin, a teacher; and Louis Wolf, a doctor. Matt Henson was the arctic expert, the one who would be their teacher. Without him they would not survive.

As they steamed up the coast of Greenland, Henson and Peary hired the best Eskimos and selected the strongest dogs. It was Matt's unhappy duty to put the unwanted Eskimos off the ship. "It is not a pleasant job to disappoint these people," he said. Before long they had 33 Eskimo families, cooking equipment, sledges, whale meat, dead walruses, 400 tons of coal, and 200 dogs on the overcrowded ship with its incredible smell.

The *Roosevelt* headed for the ice pack between

With its sharp bow and egg-shaped bottom, the *Roosevelt* was specially designed to sail through arctic ice.

Greenland and Ellesmere Island. When the ship came up against the first ice floe, Peary ordered full speed ahead. The ice cracked and split, and the *Roosevelt* steamed ahead. For more than two weeks the ship crashed and smashed its way through the ice, with Captain Bartlett roaring orders at his crew and the dogs howling at the tops of their voices. If the ice began to close in, the ship would rise like a horse taking a jump and land with a crash that splintered the ice. By September the *Roosevelt* was at Cape

Sheridan, the northern end of Ellesmere Island, its bow pointed straight toward the North Pole.

Matt's winter work went so well that he had time to visit and study navigation with Ross Marvin, who became a close friend. "I hope to perfect myself in navigation," wrote Matt. "I need to master the mathematical end." He even had time to relax in his cabin and read his favorite books by Charles Dickens.

By the end of February, they were ready to start out for the Pole. Peary went over his plan one last time. There would be a pioneer group to choose the best route and make a trail, with five small groups to follow. Every 50 to 75 miles, one of the five groups would turn back with the weakest dogs to save food for the others. It was bound to work this time.

On March 1 Matt and his team of Eskimos left to pioneer the trail to the Pole. Using his compass, Matt would choose a point in the distance. When they reached that point, he would choose another in the same direction. And so he continued, mile after mile, through shattered ice, snowstorms, and temperatures of −60°F. Each night Matt and the Eskimos fed the dogs, built a new igloo, drank warm tea and ate their frozen pemmican and biscuits, covered their eyes with a fur strap to keep out the sunlight, and slept in their furs on top of their snowshoes on top of the snow. The dogs just lay down in the snow, covered their noses with their bushy tails, and went to sleep. Each morning the men had more warm tea and pemmican. The dogs had pemmican, no tea.

By March 26 everyone had turned back but Henson and Peary, and they were stopped by the "Big Lead," the same wide river of water that had stopped them in 1902. They waited six days for strong ice to form. On April 2 Peary wrote that Matt was "again first over new ice." They crossed, and they were pinned down in their igloo for six more days by a wild, howling blizzard. On April 21 Peary took an observation of their position. They were at 87°6' north, the farthest north any expedition had ever been. They were only 175 miles from the North Pole, but the Big Lead and the storm had cost too much time. Now there was not enough food to get them to the Pole and back. In fact, there might not be enough food to get them back at all. Already, Peary wrote, dogs were eating dogs.

They headed south, with Matt leading the way. He had run the race against death before, and he had won each time.

But when they got back to the Big Lead, they saw a river a mile wide separating them from home. They could not wait for the lead to close, so they walked along the edge until they found a place where thin ice had formed over the salt water. The men crossed the ice with their feet wide apart like polar bears. Matt heard a scream of terror behind him as the Eskimos stepped onto the ice, but he couldn't turn around. He had to keep sliding his snowshoes forward across the undulating ice. If he, or anyone, fell through that transparent, fragile surface, there would be nothing to hang on to and no one to help. The horror of that long crossing seemed to go on forever, sliding, sinking, rising—yet somehow every man, every dog, every sledge crossed to safety.

They had won another battle against death, but they weren't home yet. They struggled south, climbing again over the tumbled ice blocks that they needed wings to cross but crossed anyway, until at last they reached land. The only food left was the dogs themselves, so the men ate their dogs. When they arrived at the ship at the end of May, there were only two dogs left.

And the expedition still wasn't over. The ice pack had crushed the *Roosevelt,* despite its egg-shaped bottom. The propeller and rudder were badly damaged, and there were holes in the bottom of the ship so large they had to be stuffed with packing material, tar, and cement. It was late September by the time the *Roosevelt* got to Etah, Greenland, where they left the Eskimos. On September 26 they were caught in blinding snow and a hurricane, and they still had two thousand miles of water to cross. More hurricanes ripped away the sails and rudder. As fast as the crew made a new rudder out of the ship's beams, a storm tore it away. Ice water poured through the holes in the bottom of the ship, and the crew kept packing more stuffing in the holes. Every man on board expected the ship to sink at any moment, and Captain Bartlett said he'd prefer to walk home. By the middle of October, they had run out of coal and were burning

The treacherous arctic ice
was almost too much for the
Roosevelt.

whale blubber and parts of the ship itself to power
the engine. But the *Roosevelt* stayed afloat and was
home in New York on Christmas Eve 1906. As Captain
Bartlett went to bed for the first time in weeks, he
said he was ready for the insane asylum and the ship
was ready for the trash heap. (Matt called it "a most
trying voyage.")

Peary had failed again to reach the Pole, but he
had set the world record for farthest north—Henson

and Peary and their team of Eskimos had, that is—and that was enough to win honor for Peary. Henson, now 40, and Peary, now 50, knew they couldn't keep trying forever. They would return one more time, Matt wrote, "this time to be the last, and this time to win."

In September 1907 Matt Henson married Lucy Ross. They rented a small apartment in Harlem, New York, and for the first time Matt had someone to come home to. Just one more trip, he told Lucy, and then he would be home to stay.

V
To the Pole!

Matt moved to the newly repaired *Roosevelt* to help organize the supplies for the 1908 expedition. The small ship settled lower and lower in the water as the crew carried on dynamite for blasting ice; pickaxes; shovels; guns; kerosene; and thousands of pounds of tea, coffee, dried fish, bacon, sugar, biscuits, flour, and pemmican. There were cameras, maps and charts, navigational equipment, thermometers, compasses, books, and materials for building sledges. Coal was stuffed into any space left over.

On July 6, 1908, the *Roosevelt* steamed out of New York to the sound of whistles and bells and shouts. Matt thought of Lucy. "I hoped when she next heard of me it would be with feelings of joy and happiness," he said, "and that she would be glad she had permitted me to leave her." The next day, at Oyster Bay, New York, President Theodore Roosevelt came

President Theodore Roosevelt wishes Peary luck on his sixth attempt to reach the Pole.

on board. He poked into all the corners, shook hands with all the men, cried "Bully!" and said he knew they would bring home the Pole this time. (Some folks did expect Peary to return with a pole, probably striped.) Then they were off.

Peary had selected the bravest, strongest, most intelligent men he could find for his last try. There was Matt, of course, there had to be Matt. There were

Captain Bartlett and Ross Marvin again. And there were three new men: George Borup, a young Yale graduate; Donald MacMillan, a teacher; and J. W. Goodsell, a doctor.

When MacMillan boarded the *Roosevelt,* he looked for Matt. "I had read so much about [Henson]," he said, "that naturally I studied him with interest." Matt greeted MacMillan with a handshake and a smile, and right away MacMillan saw the easy way Matt had of making friends. Later he saw Matt's courage in a terrible storm when he did the work of three men without thinking of his own safety. Donald MacMillan wrote it all down in his diary (and Matt wrote in *his* diary that he hoped he and MacMillan would become friends). In fact, all the men kept diaries of this expedition. They expected it to be successful and wanted to have the details right.

At Etah Peary learned that Dr. Cook, the same Dr. Cook who had gone north with him in 1891, was again in the Arctic, but no one knew just where. Also at Etah 41 Eskimos came aboard, and 550 tons of coal, 70 tons of whale meat, 50 dead walruses, and 246 screaming dogs were added to the overloaded ship. "The ship," Matt said, "is now in a most perfect state of dirtiness."

The *Roosevelt* arrived at Cape Sheridan on September 5, and Matt began training the new men in the art of dog driving, igloo building, and survival. He was also the interpreter. Besides all his other work, Matt made the sledges and alcohol stoves for the spring trip

Some of the 246 dogs aboard the *Roosevelt* in 1908. In addition to the dogs and whale meat and dead walruses, the 10,000 pounds of sugar took up a space 10-by-10-by-6-feet all by itself. Then there was bacon, pemmican, biscuits, coffee . . .

and sledged supplies north to Cape Columbia. On one of the trips, the cold was so awful that an Eskimo's foot began to freeze. Matt said he "thawed it out in the usual way, . . . his freezing foot under my bearskin shirt."

Between sledge trips the men lived on the ship. They ate musk ox steaks, stuffed walrus heart, and fresh bread (the cook baked 18,000 pounds of bread on this expedition). As usual, Matt ate with the crew, not with the other expedition members.

When the sun disappeared, Matt wrote, "The night is coming quickly, the long months of darkness, of quiet and cold, that...I can never get used to." The sailors played dominoes and checkers to pass the time. Some of the sailors had banjos and accordions, and the explorers often heard the song "Home Sweet Home" during that long winter.

In February 1909 they were ready to go to the Pole. Each man took one special possession—for Matt it was his Bible. Each sledge carried 450 pounds of supplies—enough pemmican, biscuits, tea, and stove alcohol to last the driver and team 50 days.

On February 28 Bartlett and Borup left Cape Columbia to pioneer the trail. At 6:30 the next morning, Henson, the leader of the main group, waited for Peary's command. At last he heard "Forward, march!" Matt's whip snapped out, and a double crack, like gunshots, cut through the silence. The eager dogs were off, yelping in their happiness.

The trail was so choppy that Matt's sledge broke. The dogs sat and rested while Matt drilled new holes and threaded sealskin lines through them, with his bare hands, to put the pieces together. Every few seconds he would have to stop and put his freezing hands under his reindeer fur jacket to warm them.

Henson and Peary caught up with Bartlett on March 4 at the Big Lead. It was as wide and fearful-looking as it had been in 1906. On March 5, still waiting beside the Big Lead, Matt saw the sun reappear, a "crimson sphere, just balanced on the brink of the world." The weather was perfect—clear with a light wind—but they could not cross the lead. Bartlett and Peary corrected their compasses, Peary paced up and down, Matt worked on the sledges, and the Eskimos worried about Tornasuk. After a few days the Eskimos were so worried that they said they were going back. Matt reminded the Eskimos that Tornasuk had never won while they were with Matt and Peary. The Eskimos agreed to stay if Matt did.

On March 11 it was clear and calm and −45°F, and the Big Lead was frozen over. The men hurried across.

On March 26, at 86°38′, it was Ross Marvin's turn to go back (three men had already returned, as planned). Henson and Marvin shook hands warmly. Marvin congratulated Matt for continuing on and wished him success in getting to the Pole.

This left Henson, Peary, Bartlett, and their teams of Eskimos. Bartlett set out again as pioneer, and on March 29 Peary and Henson caught up with him beside a wide lead. Bartlett and his team of Eskimos were asleep in their igloos, so Henson and Peary quietly built their igloos one hundred yards east of them and went to sleep. A few hours later Matt heard a great crashing and grinding. He kicked out the snow door of his igloo and saw the Arctic Ocean rolling and pitching wildly, the ice separating and huge ice blocks piling up right beside the terrified dogs. Then the ice split with the sound of a shot and zigzagged apart between Henson and Peary's igloos and Bartlett's igloos. Bartlett, his team of Eskimos, and his dogs were on a loose floating island, which began to revolve and drift into the lead, toward Matt. Bartlett had his dogs harnessed in a flash, and as the ice floe passed Matt, Bartlett, the Eskimos, and the dogs leaped across the swirling water to safety. The men were too stunned to speak. The empty igloos floated away and were gone.

On April 1, at 87°46′, it was Bartlett's turn to go back. Bartlett was disappointed at not being the one to go to the Pole with Peary, but he knew Matt Henson

The line of sledges heading toward the North Pole in March 1909

should go. Peary had told MacMillan earlier that it had to be Matt. "I can't get along without him," Peary had said.

Now it was Henson and Peary against the Arctic, as it had been for 18 years. They had only 135 miles to go; 40 strong, fresh dogs; the 4 bravest Eskimos (Ootah, Ooqueah, Egingwah, and Seegloo); and a brilliant sparkling snow highway lit by a sun that never set. Peary wrote, "My party, my equipment, and my supplies, they were perfect."

All day April 1 they repaired sledges and rested. The Eskimos had a special treat—boiled dog. At midnight April 2 Peary started out on foot in front, then rode on a sledge, as was his custom. They marched for 10 hours, and in the sunlight that night, Matt saw a marvelous sight. The full moon and the sun circled the sky opposite each other—a disk of silver and a disk of gold.

On April 3 they came to a lead covered with thin ice. As Matt drove his sledge across, the runners broke through. Matt shouted to the dogs to pull the sledge to safety, and the ice opened under his feet. He went straight down into the Arctic Ocean. It was, he said, a moment of "hideous horror." Suddenly he felt something lift him up. Ootah had raced over, grabbed Matt by the hood, and dragged him out. Matt lay in a wet, frozen heap on the ice for a few seconds, trying to get his breath back. Ootah had saved his life. "But I did not tell him so, for such occurrences are taken as part of the day's work," Matt said. Matt stripped off his wet boots, put on dry ones from the sledge, and pounded the icy water out of his furs before they could freeze solid around him. Then they hurried on.

The bitter east wind was like frozen steel, so cold that even the Eskimos complained. But the closer the group got to the top of the world, the more the shattered ice smoothed out. Peary was so anxious to reach the Pole that he would hardly stop to rest the dogs. Hour after hour, around the 24-hour day, they hurried toward the Pole. Matt could estimate mileage accurately, and on April 5 he calculated that they had marched 100 miles since Bartlett had turned back. Peary stopped and took an observation of the sun. It showed they were at 89°25′. Only 35 miles to go, he told Matt.

Before midnight on April 6 they raced off again, and at 10:00 in the morning they stopped. Matt later said, "I was driving ahead and was swinging around to the right. . . . The Commander, who was about 50′ behind, called to me and said we would go into camp. . . ." The ice was smooth and blindingly white in all directions, with patches of sapphire blue. At exactly noon Peary took his observations with the artificial horizon of warm mercury that Matt had prepared. The latitude reading showed them to be about three miles from the exact top of the world.

Matt felt tremendously proud. "I was confident that the journey had ended," he said. They had done it! He and Peary and their team of Eskimos were the *first* to reach the North Pole. He pulled off his mitten and hurried over to shake Peary's hand, but to Matt's surprise Peary turned aside. Matt decided that Peary had not seen his outstretched hand. He wrote, "I ungloved my right hand and went forward to congratulate him,...but a gust of wind blew something in his eye, or else [the pain of looking at the sun] forced him to turn aside. . . ."

At 6:00 that evening, clouds covered the sun where they were, so Peary sledged 10 miles north to take more observations. When he did so he learned that he was traveling south. To get back to camp he would travel north and then south, all in one straight line. This could only happen at the Pole.

Peary had to be absolutely sure he was in the right place, so beginning at 6:00 the next morning, he took more observations. Then he crisscrossed an area of 8-by-10 miles and took a fourth set of observations at noon.

At last Peary said, "We will plant the stars and stripes—*at the North Pole!*" Peary took a picture of Matt holding the American flag, with the Eskimos on either side also holding flags. They gave three cheers while the dogs looked on, puzzled. While Matt arranged the sledges for the journey home, Peary cut a diagonal strip from the flag and placed it in a bottle along with the record of his discovery, to leave at the top of the world. Then Peary wrote in his diary, "The Pole at last! The prize of three centuries. My dream and goal for thirty years. Mine at last!"

Matt (center) and the four Eskimos at the North Pole. Matt holds the American flag Josephine Peary made years before. It is covered with patches to replace pieces cut out and left at various "farthest north" camps.

Now they only had to get home. Peary was worn out, so Matt helped him onto a sledge. Then Matt took the group south. Although the trail was broken in places by the drifting of the ice, Matt found it far easier to travel south with light sledges than it had been to make a new trail north. Even so, he wrote, it was "17 days of haste, toil, and misery. . . . We crossed lead after lead, sometimes like a bareback rider in the circus, balancing on cake after cake of ice."

When they finally reached land, the Eskimos yelled and danced and fell onto the snow, and Ootah said, "The devil is asleep or having trouble with his wife, or we should never have come back so easily."

On April 23 they were back at Cape Columbia. When they were a day's march away from the ship, Peary hurried on ahead. Soon Matt could see the *Roosevelt* and smell hot coffee in the clear air. When Matt reached the ship, his friends rushed to greet him and pull him up the side. He was "overjoyed to find [himself] once more safe among friends." They helped Matt to his cabin, and he took off his furs and relaxed for the first time in 68 days. "When I awoke," he wrote, "I had the grandest feast imaginable set before me, and after eating, I had the most luxurious bath possible, and then some more to eat, and afterwards, some more sleep. . . . For days after I reached the *Roosevelt,* I did nothing but rest and eat."

But Matt learned that Tornasuk had been paid after all. Ross Marvin had fallen through the ice and was gone. Matt grieved for a long time over his friend.

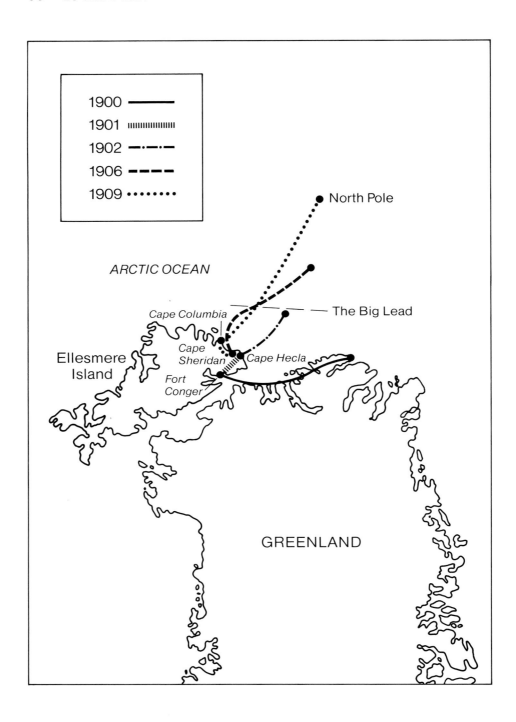

Matt was also puzzled by Peary's behavior. After they returned from the Pole, Peary didn't speak to Matt again except to give him orders. Matt said, "Not once in [three weeks] did he speak a word to me. Then he . . . ordered me to get to work. Not a word about the North Pole or anything connected with it."

On July 18, 1909, the *Roosevelt* steamed south from Cape Sheridan to Etah and arrived August 17. There, Peary and his men learned that the missing Dr. Cook had turned up safely, saying that he had been to the North Pole on April 21, 1908. Matt questioned the Eskimos who were with Cook, and they insisted they had never been out of sight of land. Peary's group decided that Cook had been joking ("We simply laughed at it," Matt said), and Peary did not hurry to report his success. He didn't reach the first radio station, at Indian Harbor, Labrador, until September 5. There, he sent a message to Mrs. Peary, "Have made good at last. I have the Pole" and "Stars and Stripes nailed to the North Pole."

But the world had heard Dr. Cook's claim just a few days before and had acclaimed *him* as the discoverer of the North Pole. When Peary landed at Battle Harbor, Newfoundland, on September 8, he learned that Cook had already been awarded a gold medal by the Royal Danish Geographical Society in Copenhagen on the basis of his claim, without any proof. Peary was stunned. There was little glory left for Robert Peary (or Matthew Henson), who had worked for 18 years to get to the Pole.

VI
After the Pole

Newspaper reporters swarmed to the *Roosevelt,* eager to hear exciting details from Peary and wire them back to the fascinated public. But Peary did not give exciting details. Sitting on a pile of fishnets, he made a flat statement giving the number of sledges, telling how the supporting parties helped, and describing how easy it finally all was. Cook's story, on the other hand, was filled with magnificent descriptions of the dangers and beauties of polar exploration. It was much more believable to the public, true or not.

Reporters crowded around Matt, hoping for more information. Matt told a *New York Times* reporter, "Dr. Cook had two inexperienced Eskimos, and he himself knew nothing about sledging over sea ice. . . . Anyone who has traveled over the land ice will tell you that a man who has had no practice sledging over the sea ice could never reach the pole. It is too

The charming Dr. Frederick Cook, pictured here in about 1936, claimed to have reached the North Pole one year before Peary. His claim to have climbed to the top of Alaska's Mount McKinley in 1906 was also disputed.

hard a proposition for an inexperienced man" (*New York Times,* September 23, 1909).

Peary retired in silence to his home on Eagle Island in Maine while waiting for scientific societies to go over his proof. He refused to make any speeches until his claim was accepted. Meanwhile the charming and likeable Dr. Cook was happily earning thousands of dollars on lecture tours, even though he still had not submitted proof to any scientific society.

William Brady, an agent, tried to get Peary to go

on a lecture tour himself. Peary refused. So Brady asked Matt and Matt agreed.

A *New York Times* article published October 19, 1909, said that people went to the Hippodrome, where Matt was speaking, to find out why Peary had chosen this "colored" man to go with him. "[There were no] doubts as to the efficiency and intelligence of Matt Henson," said the reporter. "[During] a rapid fire of questions . . . he . . . showed a quickness of mind that did much to reveal why he had so long been the explorer's trusted servant and companion. . . . [He] answered them all, always promptly, often with humor and occasionally with touches of wit. He not only showed that he knew a lot about the Arctic, but he had his facts ready for use on the spur of the moment."

Then Matt wrote his account of the discovery in his book, *A Negro Explorer at the North Pole,* and he asked Peary to write the preface. Peary agreed. He wrote, "The example and experience of Matthew Henson . . . [shows] that race, or color, or bringing-up, or environment, count nothing against a deter-mined heart, if it is backed and aided by intelligence."

By December 15 Peary's claims had been accepted by scientists appointed by the National Geographic Society and he was awarded a gold medal. Captain Bartlett was also awarded a gold medal. Matt Henson was not mentioned.

Meanwhile Dr. Cook still had not produced any proof that he had been to the North Pole, and by the end of December, the University of Copenhagen said that his claim was not supported by facts and could not be accepted.

By this time Peary and Bartlett were being honored all over Europe (except in the Scandinavian countries, home of Nansen and Sverdrup, whom Peary had offended). When Peary returned home, he went before the Naval Affairs Committee, which was considering promoting him to rear admiral. There, Peary ran into trouble. Why had he taken Henson, an uneducated black man, to the Pole rather than Bartlett?

Peary didn't tell the Committee that he took Matt because he couldn't get to the Pole without him.

Peary didn't tell the Committee what he told the American explorer, Vilhjalmur Stefansson. Matt Henson was the best, Peary said to Stefansson, "the most nearly indispensable man."

Instead Peary told the Committee that he had kept Matthew Henson with him because he had feared Matt wouldn't be able to return safely without a white man's guidance.

But the other men on the expedition knew why Peary took Matt. Donald MacMillan wrote, "Peary knew Matt Henson's real worth. . . . Highly respected by the Eskimos, he was easily the most popular man on board ship . . . Henson . . . was of more real value to our Commander than Bartlett, Marvin, Borup, Goodsell and myself all put together. Matthew Henson went to the Pole with Peary because he was a better man than any one of us."

The *Pittsburgh Dispatch* reported that Peary told the Commission he had taken only Henson in order to keep all the glory for himself. He could not bear to share the honor of discovery with another white man. Matt's part in the discovery could be, and was, dismissed.

Although Matt was unrecognized by the white world at that time (except for the men on the expedition), he was honored by the black world. In 1909 the Colored Commercial Association of Chicago presented him with a gold medal; the Boston Chamber of Commerce, a silver loving cup. On October 13, 1909, the black citizens of New York City gave a dinner in his honor at Tuxedo Hall on Madison Avenue and presented Matt with a gold watch and the thanks of the black community.

Afterword

After 1909 Robert Peary was an honored American hero, a retired naval admiral on a comfortable pension. After 1909 Matthew Henson was a parking garage attendant in Brooklyn for $16 a week. He didn't—in fact couldn't—promote himself. MacMillan said Matt was quiet and modest, and he remained so, still believing his work would prove his worth. At age 46 he became a clerk in the Customs House in New York City at a salary of $900 a year to start. He worked at the Customs House until he retired at age 70. (Peary died in 1920. Shortly before his death, Peary asked Matt to come to his bedside. Matt went immediately, and they had one last talk about their adventures together.)

Nearly 30 years after Matt returned from the Pole, some recognition came his way at last. In 1937 he was invited to join the Explorers' Club, and he often went there to visit with Bartlett and MacMillan. Matt was a popular member, respected for his wit and humor and graciousness. In 1938 he was made an honorary member of the Academy of Science and Art of Pittsburgh.

MacMillan wrote to Congress in 1938, appealing for a bill to honor Henson. MacMillan described Matt's work and the honors given to those who had done one-tenth as much. He said, "It is very evident that there is one reason only why Henson has not been honored—he is black." No bill was passed.

Howard University awarded Matt an honorary M.S. degree in 1939. On January 28, 1944, Congress authorized a medal for all the men on the expedition, including Matthew Henson. The following year Matt received his silver medal for "outstanding service to the Government of the United States . . . for exceptional fortitude, superb seamanship, and fearless determination. . . ."

In 1948 the Geographic Society of Chicago gave a

Matt and Lucy Henson with President Eisenhower at the White House on the 45th anniversary of the discovery of the North Pole. Matt is pointing to the Arctic on the globe.

banquet in Matt's honor, with more than one thousand people attending. MacMillan, now an admiral himself, presented Matt with a gold medal on which were engraved the words "'I can't get along without him.' Peary." In 1949 Matt was invited to Washington to celebrate the fortieth anniversary of the discovery, but he wasn't well enough to go. However, in 1954, at age 87, he went to Washington, laid a wreath on Peary's grave, and went to the White House to meet President Eisenhower.

In 1955 Matt Henson died. He was buried in a simple grave at Woodlawn Cemetery in the Bronx, New York.

But Matt's work continued to prove his worth. In 1959, April 6 was proclaimed "Matthew Henson Day" in Maryland. In 1961 Maryland honored him with a plaque in the State House at Annapolis. It said, "Matthew Alexander Henson, Co-Discoverer of the North Pole with Admiral Robert Edwin Peary, April 6, 1909 . . . exemplification of courage, fortitude and patriotism . . . established everlasting prestige and glory for his state and country." In 1963 Baltimore named its newest elementary school the Matthew A. Henson School.

On April 6, 1988, Matthew Alexander Henson, co-discoverer of the North Pole, was reburied in Arlington National Cemetery beside Admiral Peary. The final wrong was made right.

Bibliography

Primary Sources:

Bartlett, Robert. *The Log of Bob Bartlett.* New York, London: G.P. Putnam's Sons, 1928.

Borup, George. *A Tenderfoot with Peary.* New York: Frederick A. Stokes, 1911.

Goodsell, John. *On Polar Trails: the Peary Expedition to the North Pole, 1908-09.* Austin: Eakin Press, 1983.

Henson, Matthew. *A Negro Explorer at the North Pole.* New York: Frederick A. Stokes, 1912.

MacMillan, Donald. *How Peary Reached the Pole.* Boston: Houghton Mifflin Company, 1934.

Peary, Josephine. *My Arctic Journal.* New York: Contemporary Publishing Co., 1893.

Peary, Robert E. *Nearest the Pole.* New York: Doubleday & Co., 1907.

Peary, Robert E. *The North Pole.* New York: Frederick A. Stokes, 1910.

Peary, Robert E. *Northward Over the Great Ice.* New York: Frederick A. Stokes, 1898.

Secondary Sources:

Angell, Pauline. *To the Top of the World: The Story of Peary and Henson.* New York: Rand McNally & Company, 1964.

Brawley, Benjamin. *Negro Builders and Heroes.* Chapel Hill: University of North Carolina Press, 1937.

Dolan, Edward. *Matthew Henson, Black Explorer.* New York: Dodd, Mead, 1979.

Hobbs, William H. *Peary.* New York: Macmillan, Inc., 1936.

Hunt, William R. *To Stand at the Pole.* New York: Stein and Day, 1981.

Miller, Floyd. *Ahdoolo!* New York: E.P. Dutton, 1963.

Robinson, Bradley. *Dark Companion.* New York: Robert M. McBride, 1947.

Weems, John Edward. *Peary: The Explorer and the Man.* Boston: Houghton Mifflin Company, 1967.

All quotations in this biography were taken from the above sources.

Index

The illustrations are reproduced through the courtesy of: pp. 2, 6, 13, The Department of Rare
Books and Special Collections, The University of Michigan Library; pp. 16, 33, 57, The Peary
Collection, © National Geographic Society; pp. 21, 26, 36, 60, Dartmouth College Library;
pp. 23, 48, 52, 55, The Peary-MacMillan Arctic Museum and Arctic Studies Center, Bowdoin
College; pp. 8, 43, 64, 69, the National Archives; p. 74, Dwight D. Eisenhower Library, National
Park Services. Cover photographs courtesy of the National Archives (black-and-white) and
Steve McCutcheon (color).

921
HEN

Ferris, Jeri

Arctic explorer

C.2

921
HEN

Ferris, Jeri

Arctic explorer

C.2

$9.95

DATE	BORROWER'S NAME		
1-11-1902	Matt Henson	1-30-1902	
5-02-1902	Crosin Torres	5-20-1902	